D1199190

BIGGEST, BADDEST BOOK OF

SPACE

JEN SCHOELLER

Consulting Editor, Diane Craig, M.A./Reading Specialist

Super Sandcastle

An Imprint of Abdo Publishing
www.abdopublishing.com

www.abdopublishing.com

Published by Abdo Publishing, a division of ABDO, PO Box 398166, Minneapolis, Minnesota 55439. Copyright © 2015 by Abdo Consulting Group, Inc. International copyrights reserved in all countries. No part of this book may be reproduced in any form without written permission from the publisher. Super SandCastle™ is a trademark and logo of Abdo Publishing.

Printed in the United States of America, North Mankato, Minnesota
102014
012015

THIS BOOK CONTAINS
RECYCLED MATERIALS

Editor: Alex Kuskowski
Content Developer: Nancy Tuminelly
Interior Design and Production: Jen Schoeller, Mighty Media, Inc.
Cover Design: Anders Hansen, Mighty Media, Inc.
Photo Credits: Shutterstock, Wikipedia Commons, Nasa

Library of Congress Cataloging-in-Publication Data

Schoeller, Jen.
 Biggest, baddest book of space / Jen Schoeller.
    pages cm. -- (Biggest, baddest books)
 ISBN 978-1-62403-518-0
1. Astronomy--Juvenile literature. 2. Space--Juvenile literature. I. Title.
 QB46.S32 2015
 520--dc23
                    2014024011

Super SandCastle™ books are created by a team of professional educators, reading specialists, and content developers around five essential components—phonemic awareness, phonics, vocabulary, text comprehension, and fluency—to assist young readers as they develop reading skills and strategies and increase their general knowledge. All books are written, reviewed, and leveled for guided reading, early reading intervention, and Accelerated Reader® programs for use in shared, guided, and independent reading and writing activities to support a balanced approach to literacy instruction.

CONTENTS

OUTER SPACE

Outer space is the area around the Earth. Space is unbelievably huge. The planets, stars, moons, and other space objects are in space.

Space is very cold. It is measured using the Kelvin scale. It is 2.7 **degrees** Kelvin. That is minus 455 degrees Fahrenheit (–270 C)!

EARTH'S ATMOSPHERE

EXOSPHERE

MOON

UPPER ATMOSPHERE

THERMOSPHERE

INTERNATIONAL SPACE STATION

MESOSPHERE

MIDDLE ATMOSPHERE

METEORS

STRATOSPHERE

AIRPLANES

TROPOSPHERE

LOWER ATMOSPHERE

HOT AIR BALLON

SOLAR SYSTEM

O ur solar system is the sun and everything that orbits it. That includes eight planets. Earth is the third planet from the sun.

MARS

DIAMETER: *4,212 mi. (6,779 km)*

ORBIT PERIOD: *687 days*

MERCURY

DIAMETER: *3,032 mi. (4,879 km)*

ORBIT PERIOD: *88 days*

EARTH

DIAMETER: *7,918 mi. (12,742 km)*

ORBIT PERIOD: *365 days*

VENUS

DIAMETER: *7,521 mi. (12,104 km)*

ORBIT PERIOD: *225 days*

THE SUN

The sun is a star.

NEPTUNE

DIAMETER: *30,599 mi. (49,244 km)*

ORBIT PERIOD: *165 years*

JUPITER

DIAMETER: *86,881 mi. (139,822 km)*

ORBIT PERIOD: *12 years*

URANUS

DIAMETER: *31,518 mi. (50,724 km)*

ORBIT PERIOD: *84 years*

SATURN

DIAMETER: *72,367 mi. (116,464 km)*

ORBIT PERIOD: *29 years*

ASTEROID BELT

An asteroid belt has rocks, metals, and other objects.

FUN IN THE SUN

The sun is the center of the solar system. It provides heat and light. The heat and light let life exist on Earth. The other planets are too close or too far away. Some get too much heat and light. The others don't get enough.

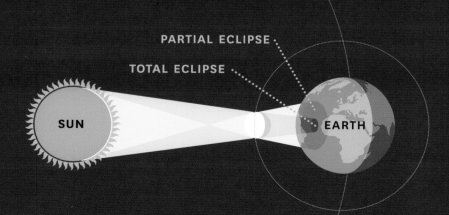

PARTIAL ECLIPSE

TOTAL ECLIPSE

SUN

EARTH

SOLAR ECLIPSE

Sometimes the moon gets between the sun and Earth. It blocks the sun's light. That is an eclipse. A total eclipse lasts 5 to 7 minutes.

SUN

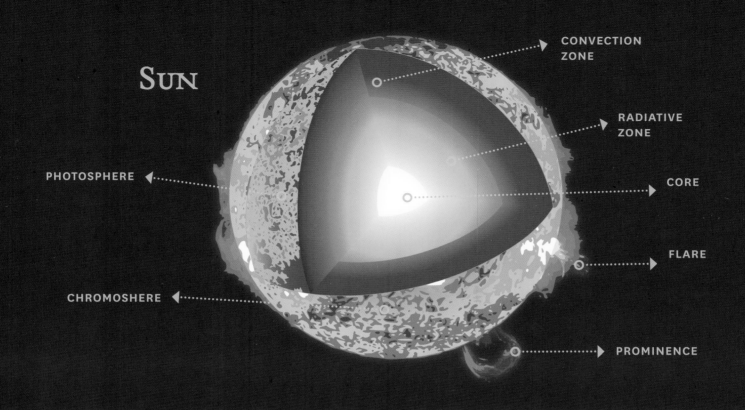

CONVECTION ZONE

RADIATIVE ZONE

CORE

FLARE

PROMINENCE

PHOTOSPHERE

CHROMOSHERE

WHAT IS IT MADE OF?

73% HYDROGEN

25% HELIUM

2% CARBON, OXYGEN, IRON

ONE
million earths
CAN FIT INSIDE
THE SUN

THE SUN ☀ is
4.5
BILLION
years old

COOL PLANETS

WATER ON MARS

In the 1960s, scientists started sending missions to Mars. They found signs that Mars once had a lot of water. But most of it is gone or frozen now. The most recent rover sent to Mars is Curiosity. It landed on Mars in 2012.

JUPITER'S HURRICANE

Jupiter has a large spot on it. It's called the Great Red Spot. The spot is a storm like a hurricane. It has lasted 200 to 300 years!

SATURN CAN FLOAT!

Saturn is the second-largest planet. It is also the lightest planet. If Saturn could fit in a pool, it would float!

The MILKY WAY

A galaxy is huge. It includes stars, planets, and other space objects. There are **billions** of galaxies in the universe. Each galaxy has between 10 million and 100 **trillion** stars.

Our solar system is in the Milky Way galaxy. It has 100 to 400 billion stars. It is shaped like a flat **spiral**.

THE MILKY WAY LOOKS LIKE A BAND OF LIGHT IN THE SKY.

DISTANCE TRAVELED BY LIGHT IN 80,000 YEARS

PERSEUS ARM

ORION SPUR

YOU ARE HERE

OUTER ARM

NORMA ARM

NEAR 3-KPC ARM

GALACTIC BAR

EARTH'S ORBIT THROUGH THE GALAXY

SAGITTARIUS ARM

FAR 3-KPC ARM

SCUTUM-CENTAURUS ARM

SUPERMASSIVE
BLACK HOLE

THE LIFE OF A STAR

Most stars are **billions** of years old. But they don't stay the same. They have a life cycle. A star starts as a cloud of **hydrogen**. Gravity pulls the hydrogen together. It becomes an average star or a massive star. Each type goes through different stages.

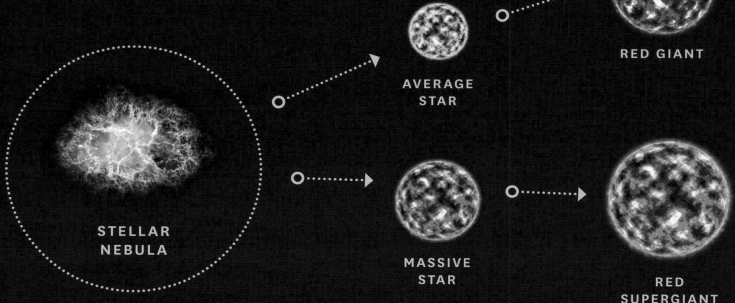

STELLAR NEBULA

AVERAGE STAR

RED GIANT

MASSIVE STAR

RED SUPERGIANT

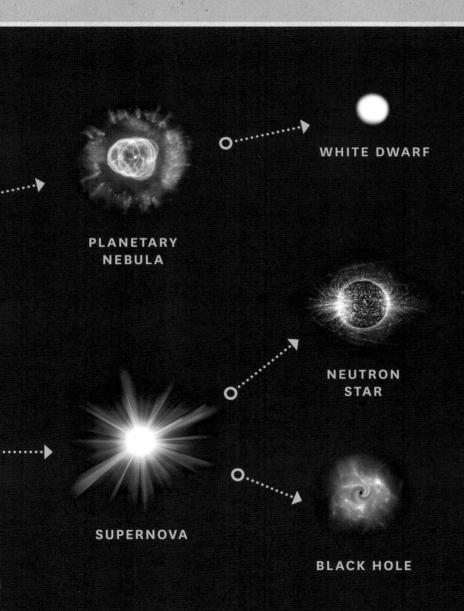

PLANETARY
NEBULA

WHITE DWARF

SUPERNOVA

NEUTRON
STAR

BLACK HOLE

REAL SHOOTING STARS

Most stars move
around the galaxy. But
some stars move much faster
than others. Scientists think
they were shot out of the
galaxy's center.

Flying SPACE ROCKS

ASTEROIDS

Asteroids orbit the sun. They are made of rock and metal. Most asteroids are in a long group. It's called an asteroid belt.

COMETS

A comet is a ball of frozen gas, rock, and dust. It orbits the sun. It gets warm when it is near the sun. The gases melt. This creates a bright **streak** of light. It's called a coma.

METEOROIDS

A meteoroid is a rock. Meteoroids can be as small as specks of dust. Or they can be as big as buildings. They move through space at different speeds. The fastest ones go 160,000 miles per hour (257,495 kmh)!

IRON METEOROID

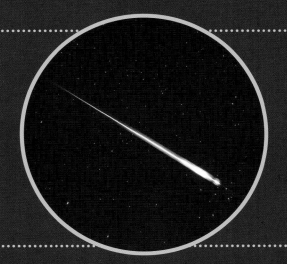

METEORS

Some meteoroids fly toward Earth. They burn up in Earth's atmosphere. Then they become meteors. A meteor has a bright tail of light.

METEORITES

Some meteors hit the Earth's surface. They are called meteorites. Thousands of meteorites have been found on Earth.

IRON METEORITE FOUND IN WOLFE CREEK, AUSTRALIA

THE POINT OF

A black hole is an area of space. It has a lot of gravity. The gravity is so strong that not even light can escape.

The boundary of the gravity is called the event horizon. Anything inside it will fall into the black hole.

The center of the black hole is called the singularity.

THE EVENT HORIZON

SINGULARITY

NO RETURN BLACK HOLES

Supermassive Black Holes

Supermassive black holes are the biggest black holes. They are **billions** of times bigger than the sun. Many galaxies have supermassive black holes in their centers. Scientists aren't sure how they are created.

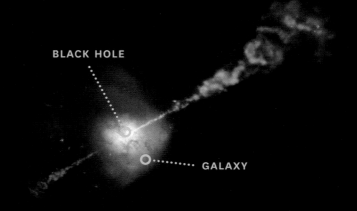

BLACK HOLE

GALAXY

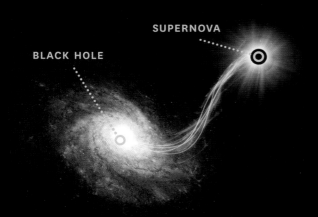

SUPERNOVA

BLACK HOLE

Stellar Mass Black Holes

Stellar mass black holes come from dying stars. Sometimes big stars burn up. Then they explode. This is called a supernova. Anything left after the supernova sticks together in a tight ball. That is a black hole.

OUR EVER-EXPANDING

□········□

WHAT IS THE UNIVERSE?

The universe is everything that exists. It includes galaxies, stars, and planets. It includes light and energy.

BIG BANG THEORY

The Big Bang is how the universe formed. It started as a single point. Then it grew very quickly. It grew 90 times its size in less than a second! Then it started growing more slowly. The universe is still growing today.

□········□

UNIVERSE

HOW BIG IS THE UNIVERSE?

No one knows. Scientists can see only 46 **billion** light-years away. A light-year is how far light travels in one year. One light-year is about 6 **trillion** miles (9.5 trillion km).

HOW OLD IS THE UNIVERSE?

The universe is about 13.7 billion years old. That is when the Big Bang happened.

The Future Of SPACE EXPLORATION

NASA is planning another mission to the moon. They want an astronaut to walk on the moon by 2020. Then they will send people to Mars and other planets.

The first step is building better spacecraft. NASA is working on Orion crew exploration **vehicles**. They are space **capsules** that can hold four people.

INTERNATIONAL SPACE STATION

Orion capsules will take crew to and from the International Space Station.

WHAT DO YOU KNOW ABOUT SPACE?

1. THE CURIOSITY ROVER LANDED ON MARS IN 2012. **TRUE OR FALSE?**

2. A STAR STAYS THE SAME FOR **BILLIONS** OF YEARS. **TRUE OR FALSE?**

3. ASTEROIDS ARE MADE OF PLASTIC. **TRUE OR FALSE?**

4. THE SINGULARITY IS THE CENTER OF A BLACK HOLE. **TRUE OR FALSE?**

ANSWERS: 1) TRUE 2) FALSE 3) FALSE 4) TRUE

GLOSSARY

BILLION – a very large number. One billion is also written 1,000,000,000.

CAPSULE – the part of a spacecraft where the astronauts are.

DEGREE – the unit used to measure temperature.

HYDROGEN – a chemical element that is a colorless, odorless gas.

SPIRAL – a pattern that winds in a circle.

STREAK – a long, thin mark or stripe.

TRILLION – a very large number. One trillion is also written 1,000,000,000,000.

VEHICLE – something used to carry persons or large objects. Examples include cars, trucks, boats, and bicycles.